This Book Belongs To

- -

- -

- -

Copyright Page

This Activity book
©2021 Shaaim Family LLC

All rights reserved. No portion of this book may be reproduced, stored in a retrieval system or transmitted an any for or by any means -electronic, mechanical, photocopy, recording, or any other – except for brief quotation in printed reviews, without the permission of the publisher.

Published by: Our Communities Our Children Publishing LLC, 1205 Atlantic Avenue, Brooklyn, N.Y. 11216
Website: www.OCOCbooks.com
A children's history book about ancient Egypt (Kemet).
Author: Obi Shaaim Maa
Cover: Metu Degg Khet
Graphics: Metu Degg Khet
ISBN: 978-1-953952-19-6

Description

Kheru Nefer Kings and Queens Activity Book

Help your child continue his journey through history. This Activity Book is designed to by used with the Kheru Nefer: Beautiful Night (Kings and Queens) history book for ages 11 to 14. It will help deepen your child's recognition and understanding of the greatest kings and queens of ancient Egypt (Kemet). It will also strengthen his vocabulary, glossary and reading skills. He'll have the opportunity to answer questions about historical events, explore personal names and examine hieroglyphic symbols related to Egypt's royal couples. This book is for Advanced readers, estimated ages 11 to 14. But if you believe your child can use this book, give it to him, no matter his age.

Kings and Queens Hieroglyph Match

Draw a line from the king's or queen's picture to their name and hieroglyph.

Ahmose

Ahmes
Ah-Ms
(Moon Child)

Ahmose-Nefertari

Ahmes Nefertari
Ah-Ms Nfrtri
(Moon Childs beautiful companion)

Narmer

Narmer
NrMr
(fierce catfish)

Neithhotep

Neith-Hetep
Nth-Htp
(Neith is at peace)

Mentuhotep I

Mentu-Hetep
Mntu-Htp
(Mentu is at peace)

Neferu I

Nefer Ru
Nfru
(Beautifuly great)

Kings and Queens Hieroglyph Match

Draw a line from the king's or queen's picture to their name and hieroglyph.

Hatshepsut

Hat-Shepsut
Ht Shpst
(Formost of Shepsut)

Thutmose II

Tehuti Mes
Thti Ms
(Tehuti's Child)

Amenhotep III

Amen-hetep (hotep)
Amn-htp
(Amen is at peace)

Tiye

Tie-yee
Tiye
(Sovereign)

Senusret III

Sen-nu-sret
Usrt-Sn
(Powerful Brother)

Neferthenut

Nefert HeNut
Nfrt-hnt
(Beautifuly Serving Nut)

Kings and Queens Hieroglyph Match

Draw a line from the king's or queen's picture to their name and hieroglyph.

Thutmose I

Tehuti-Mes
Thti-Ms
(Tehuti's Child)

Queen Ahmose

Ahmes
Ah-Ms
(Moon's Child)

Khufu

Koo-Fu
Khufu
(Protector)

Henutsen

Hen-nut-sen
HNutSen
(Sister Wife)

Djoser

Zosar
Djsr
(Sacred)

Hetephernebti

Hetep-her-nebti
Htp-hr-nbti
(Peace upon the provider)

Kings and Queens Hieroglyph Match

Draw a line from the king's or queen's picture to their name and hieroglyph.

Senusret I

Sen-nu-Useret
Usrt-Sn
(Powerful Brother)

Neferu III

Nefer u
Nfru
(Beautifuly Great)

Thutmose I

Tehuti-Mes
Thti-Ms
(Tehuti's Child)

Merytre-Hatshepsut I

Merut Ra-Hat-Shepsut
Mrut-Ra-Ht-Shpst
(Beloved of Ra
Formost of Shepsut)

Historical Events Match

Use the Kheru Nefer: Beautiful Night (Kings and Queens) Ages 7 to 10/ Ages 11 to 14.

Draw a line from their picture to the correct thing they did in history.

Mentuhotep and Neferu

Built halls and monuments

Hatshepsut and Thutmose II

Defeated the Hyksos

Ahmose/Ahmose Nefertiti

Subdued invaders and warlords

Historical Events Match

Use the Kheru Nefer: Beautiful Night (Kings and Queens) Ages 7 to 10/ Ages 11 to 14.

Draw a line from their picture to the correct thing they did in history.

Narmer and Neithhotep

Architects of the Great Pyramid

Kufu and Henutsen

Revived trade and prosperity

Senusret III and Neferhenut

International power reach its peak

Amen Hetep III and Tyie

Unified the "Two Lands"

Historical Events Match

Use the Kheru Nefer: Beautiful Night (Kings and Queens) Ages 7 to 10/ Ages 11 to 14.

<u>Draw a line from their picture to the correct thing they did in history.</u>

Thutmose I and Queen Ahmose

Invented the Step Pyramid

Thutmose III Merytre Hatshepsut

Conquered territories

Djoser and Hetephernebti

Defeated the Hyksos

Senusret and Neferu III

Built tombs and temples

Kings and Queens Glossary Match (Ages 11 to 14)

Use the Kheru Nefer: Beautiful Night (Kings and Queens) Ages 11 to 14 glossary
<u>Put the letter of the word next to the correct definition</u>.

A. Abound/Abounded
B. Ancient Egypt
C. Army
D. Build
E. Chase/Chased
F. Conceive/Conceived
G. Construct/Constructed

____A group of men and women who fight for a country.

____To make something.

____A seven thousand year old country in east Africa.

____To make something or someone go away.

____To think of and imagine something before making it real.

____To make or build

____To be all over and everywhere.

Kings and Queens Glossary Match (Ages 11 to 14)

Use the Kheru Nefer: Beautiful Night (Kings and Queens) Ages 11 to 14 glossary
<u>Put the letter of the word next to the correct definition</u> .

A. Country
B. Create
C. Culture
D. Defeat
E. Erected
F. Expand/Expanded
G. Force/Forced
H. Guarantee/Guaranteed

____To make or build a large building or thing.

____To make something.

____To know or be sure of something.

____To lose or make someone lose.

____Land that people make their own.

____To become big or bigger.

____To make something or someone do something.

____A way of living.

Kings and Queens Glossary Match (Ages 11 to 14)

Use the Kheru Nefer: Beautiful Night (Kings and Queens) Ages 11 to 14 glossary
<u>Put the letter of the word next to the correct definition</u> .

A. Gigantic
B. Grand
C. Great
D. Grow
E. Health/Healthy
F. Increase/Increased
G. Invader/Invaders
H. King

___ Male or man ruler of a nation, people or group.

___ Big or important.

___ People or things that come to a place where they do not belong and are not wanted.

___ When your body is strong.

___ Big or important.

___ To make more.

___ Big.

Kings and Queens Glossary Match (Ages 11 to 14)

Use the Kheru Nefer: Beautiful Night (Kings and Queens) Ages 11 to 14 glossary
<u>Put the letter of the word next to the correct definition</u>.

A. Large
B. Magnificence
C. Military
D. Monuments
E. Nation
F. Obelisk/Obelisks
G. Obvious
H. Occupiers

____Big buildings or statues to show someone or something important.

____A country or people with laws

____A long, tall pyramid type building.

____A group of people who fight. An army.

____Big.

____Someone who holds and lives on someone's land.

____Big.

____Something can be seen.

Kings and Queens Glossary Match (Ages 11 to 14)

Use the Kheru Nefer: Beautiful Night (Kings and Queens) Ages 11 to 14 glossary
<u>Put the letter of the word next to the correct definition</u>.

A. Oppose/Opposed
B. Order
C. Peace
D. Peak
E. Penetrate/Penetrated
F. Power
G. Presented
H. Prosperous

____To have everything you need.

____The ability to make someone do what you want.

____Things and people are in the right place and doing the right things.

____When people do not fight.

____The top or the greatest.

____To show something.

____To be against something or someone.

____To put people or things into something or into a place.

Kings and Queens Glossary Match (Ages 11 to 14)

Use the Kheru Nefer: Beautiful Night (Kings and Queens) Ages 11 to 14 glossary
<u>Put the letter of the word next to the correct definition</u>.

A. Pyramid
B. Queen
C. Raised
D. Rectitude
E. Region
F. Reign
G. Retreat: To make someone go back or go away.

____ A big three-sided building used as a tomb.

____ To be good and live right.

____ To make someone go back or go away.

____ Female or woman ruler of a nation, people or group.

____ To get something.

____ To rule or govern.

____ Land.

Kings and Queens Glossary Match (Ages 11 to 14)

Use the Kheru Nefer: Beautiful Night (Kings and Queens) Ages 11 to 14 glossary
<u>Put the letter of the word next to the correct definition</u>.

A. Revive

B. Rich/Richest

C. Ruler

D. Seasons

E. Secure: To make safe.

F. Security: To make and be safe.

G. Servitude

____ One who serves and controls a nation, people or group.

____ To do what someone else says.

____ To make and be safe.

____ To bring back to life.

____ To have all the things you need.

____ Spring, summer, fall and winter.

____ To make safe.

Kings and Queens Glossary Match (Ages 11 to 14)

Use the Kheru Nefer: Beautiful Night (Kings and Queens) Ages 11 to 14 glossary
<u>Put the letter of the word next to the correct definition</u>.

A. Subdue/Subdued
B. Superpower
C. Temple
D. Territories
E. Tomb
F. Tower/Towered
G. Trade
H. Undertook

____ To do something.
____ Strong nation.
____ To hold or control.
____ Lands.
____ A place for the dead.
____ A place where people pray.
____ To give something important and get something important in return.
____ To be bigger than something or someone.

Kings and Queens Glossary Match (Ages 11 to 14)

Use the Kheru Nefer: Beautiful Night (Kings and Queens) Ages 11 to 14 glossary Put the letter of the word next to the correct definition.

A. Unified
B. Unifiers
C. Warriors
D. Wealthy
E. Withstand
F. Wrangled
G. Zenith

____ Fighters.

____ When people have everything that they need.

____ To take something.

____ Getting people to work together.

____ The top or the greatest.

____ Being and working together.

____ To stay up.

Kings and Queens Name Questions

Use the <u>Hieroglyph Match</u> page in this book to answer the following questions.

1. What is the meaning of Narmer's name?

   _____

2. Why do you think they called him that?

   _____

3. What is the meaning of the name Ahmose?

   _____

Kings and Queens Name Questions

Use the <u>Hieroglyph Match</u> page in this book to answer the following questions.

1. Whose name means "Beautifully Great?"
   _____

2. What is the meaning of "Amenhotep?"
   _____

3. Whose name means "Protector?"
   _____

Kings and Queens Name Questions

Use the <u>Hieroglyph Match</u> page in this book to answer the following questions.

1. Why do you think they called him "Protector?"

   _____

2. How many kings had the name "Powerful Brother?"

   _____

3. What is the meaning of Tyie's name?

   _____

4. Why do you think the Egyptians wrote with pictures (Hieroglyphs)?

   _____

Kheru Nefer: Beautiful Night: (Kings and Queens) is history, music, dance and art packaged in the patterned, predictable and rhythmic harmonies of a fun-filled children's book.
This addition to the Kheru Nefer: Beautiful Night series features 11 king and queen pairs who held their relationships together in order to hold a nation together.
Their enduring accomplishments are brought back so your child (Children) can enjoy and learn.
To get the the childrens history book and other Kheru Nefer products, go to:

OCOCBooks.com or your favorite online book store.

Kheru Nefer means Beautiful Night

Thank you

www.ingramcontent.com/pod-product-compliance
Lightning Source LLC
Chambersburg PA
CBHW081312070526
44578CB00006B/855